What Should I Do?

~

Six True Adventures from Orleans History

Is it as plainly in our living shown
By slant and twist, which way which the wind hath blown?

Adelaide Crapsey,
On Seeing Weather-beaten trees

What Should I Do?

~

Six True Adventures from Orleans History

by

June Chandler Fletcher

Illustrated by

Elizabeth Hayes Pratt

Snow Library Publications

Orleans, Massachusetts

Library of Congress Catalog Card No. 96-68465

ISBN 0-9651-393-1-X

First Edition

Prologue

~

ORLEANS, CAPE COD. Where did we get these names?

When Leif Ericson saw Nauset Beach in 1003, he called it Furdustrandir, which means "the Wonderlands." In 1602, six hundred years later, an Englishman named Bartholomew Gosnold came to the Cape's shores. His crew were so glad to be on dry land after two months at sea that they called the land "Shoal Hope." But they caught so many codfish that they soon changed the name to Cape Cod. (Which is easier to say, isn't it?)

In 1651 a large tract of land on Cape Cod named Nauset became the town of Eastham. It was the only town beyond Yarmouth until Harwich became a town in 1694. Further north, Wellfleet set off and established a boundary with Eastham in 1763, becoming a town in its own right.

Finally, in 1797 a group of men voted to have Eastham's South Parish become a smaller separate town which would be easier to manage. The town would run from Brewster on the southwest to Rock Creek, through Town Cove and Nauset Harbor on the north.

But what to name the new town?

A committee consisting of Isaac Snow and two other townsmen was formed to select a name. The three couldn't agree, so the committee was enlarged to eight. (Usually when you increase the size of a committee, it's even harder to agree!)

Isaac and several other men had fought in the Revolutionary War against the English and couldn't abide the thought of giving the town an English name. But Isaac had met Louis Philippe, the Duke of Orléans, in France. The Duke came to New England in 1797 to escape the terror of the French Revolution. He believed in democracy and was very popular here. So the committee decided to name our town Orleans after the French Duke.

Whether under the name of Eastham during its first 140 years, or Orleans ever since, our town has been home to strong and adventurous spirits. The true tales that follow span four hundred years. The first two happened while Orleans was still part of Eastham. "Eastham/Orleans" refers to our town before 1797.

Each adventure is told in the first person. If these narrators could speak today, here's what they might tell you.

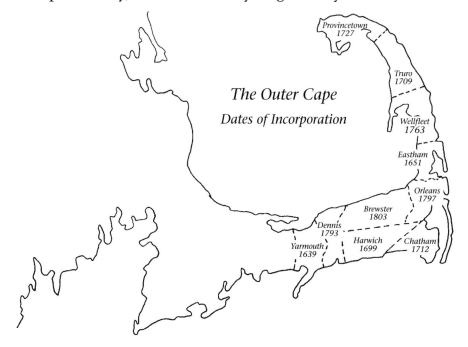

The Outer Cape

Dates of Incorporation

Provincetown
1727

Truro
1709

Wellfleet
1763

Eastham
1651

Orleans
1797

Brewster
1803

Dennis
1793

Harwich
1699

Chatham
1712

Yarmouth
1639

John Billington, Jr.

~

Y NAME IS JOHN BILLINGTON, JUNIOR. I was born in 1613. I was but seven years old when I came to Cape Cod on the *Mayflower*. My elder brother Francis and I were considered naughty children and were often rebuked and thrashed. Methinks we just had a lot of curiosity.

One day when the men had gone ashore on the bay side of Cape Cod seeking a good site for our settlement, Francis shot off some muskets to frighten the women and girls. I set off squibs, which were little pieces of gunpowder wrapped in paper. That was a great joke. The girls were really frightened, but the grown-ups were most angry. They claimed we almost blew up the *Mayflower*! But my most lively adventure came after we Pilgrims settled in Plymouth, and it took place in Eastham/Orleans.

Wherever our *Mayflower* group tried to land and explore, the Indians had shot their bows and arrows against them. 'Tis true, I can't blame the Indians much. Some of our people had stolen corn that the Indians had buried in mounds for the winter. Also, a few years before our landing, Captain Stanley Hunt had kidnapped twenty-seven Indians, including two who were named Squanto and Samoset, in order to sell them in Spain.

Squanto escaped from his kidnappers and hid in a boat for England. He was helped by an Englishman to return to America.

Samoset also escaped and was an astonishment to our group in Plymouth when he came to welcome us, speaking English!

But it was Squanto who saved my life.

Our first winter in Plymouth was most hard. People became ill and half of our settlers died. But we Billingtons stayed well and cared for the sick all winter long.

When spring came, Francis went with the men to do men's work and I, as usual, was left behind.

What should I do?

Restless for adventure, I started south on a long, rambling walk through the woods. Trouble was, I became lost. I was

affrighted and hungry and ate lots of partridge berries and wintergreen herbs, and then fell asleep. When I awakened, it was dark. I was in a dreadful fright. For the next four days I wandered in the woods, eating berries with my stomach growing emptier every day.

When I woke up on the fifth morning, an Indian was bending over me. I was most terrified! He and another Indian took me in their canoe to their village. They were from the Nauset tribe and lived in what is now Orleans. They were very good to me. They fed me baked fish and corn meal cakes which tasted overly much better than anything I'd ever eaten!

I learned interesting things about the Nauset Indians. Their leader was Sachem Aspinet. He was most kind to me and decked me out in wampum, the polished beads and shells they used for money. He was also good to his tribe. He took care of the squaws whose husbands had died and also for old Nausets who couldn't hunt or fish any longer. He settled any tribal arguments fairly.

I had great delight playing with the Indian children! They were most interested in my odd, torn clothes. Life with the Nausets was such joy that I wondered why I had been so afeared when one of them found me.

After a week I saw the Pilgrim's small boat, called a shallop coming from the ocean toward the Indian village. Our Governor Bradford had asked Squanto and his Indians to help find me. The governor was glad I was with Aspinet because he wanted to repay the Indians for the corn that his men had taken from them in December. That was when the Pilgrims first landed on Cape Cod and ravaged the supply the Indians had saved for winter.

Aspinet and the Nausets remained friendly and helpful to our little Plymouth colony. Another winter they brought us corn and beans from Eastham/Orleans when we were almost starving.

Six years after the Nausets rescued me, when the English ship *Sparrowhawk* carrying colonists to Virginia stranded on Nauset beach, an Indian runner was sent to Plymouth. He informed Governor Bradford that other white men were on the Cape and needed help. This probably saved the lives of the *Sparrowhawk* passengers.

But my life's greatest adventure was with the Nausets. I was always grateful for their friendship and for saving my life when I was but a curious seven-year-old child.

~

*J*OHN *BILLINGTON JR.'S LUCK DID NOT LAST. He died of gangrene a few years before his father, John Billington Senior, became the only Pilgrim to be hanged in the new colony. Billington Senior was found guilty of killing a new arrival in Plymouth after a violent quarrel.*

Except for Squanto, his entire tribe died in the plague of 1617. He then joined the Pilgrims in Plymouth. Sachem Aspinet signed a pact saying he was a loyal subject of King James, and the Pilgrims considered him kind and noble. A few years later, however, when there was an uprising among some Indians, Myles Standish and his troops mistakenly thought Aspinet and the Nausets were conspiring against the English. The Nausets were so frightened by the quick-tempered Standish that Aspinet and his leaders hid in unhealthy swamps to escape Standish and his attacks. Aspinet died in a swamp in 1623.

The Sparrowhawk's *skeletal remains were found on Nauset Beach 237 years later, in 1863.*

During the 1700s and 1800s more than three thousand vessels sank on the forty miles of the Cape's outer shore. Every year pieces of these ancient shipwrecks are uncovered by the shifting sands and tides. Have you found a piece yet?

Samuel Bellamy

~

MY NAME IS SAMUEL BELLAMY. I was born around 1690 in England. The biggest adventure of my life, which killed me, took place partly in Eastham/Orleans.

When I was just a young English sailor, I decided to find fortune in the new world. I also wanted to find some relatives who had settled on Cape Cod. In an old sloop I made it to Eastham/Orleans, where I stayed at Higgins Tavern.

While there I met Maria Hallett who was fifteen years old—and could she sing like a bird! We fell in love, but had no money to marry.

I wanted to search for treasure and make my fortune in the Caribbean. A Spanish fleet had sunk there some years before, and it was rumored there was wealth to be had for the taking. I said a tearful farewell to Maria and promised to return with a fortune and make her a princess of an island in the West Indies. Maria promised to wait for me, and she did.

I needed a backer for my trip and took on Paulsgrave Williams who was a goldsmith in Rhode Island. Like me, he wanted adventure and treasure.

We ran our ship as a true democracy. Each member had one vote and all decisions were made according to the number of votes cast. When we reached the Caribbean, we learned to our sorrow that many, many other treasure seekers had beaten us to it, and there was nothing left for us.

What should I do?

Go home empty-handed, or "go on account"—which meant becoming a pirate? Though I sorely missed my Maria, I finally decided to "go on account" and Williams and most of the crew agreed. After all, practically all of them had been treated brutally on the merchant vessels they had once sweated on for a pittance. Now we would try to take over these merchant vessels. It would be sweet revenge for these sailors to capture such ships and grow rich by selling their cargoes!

Also, many of my men and other pirates had once been privateers. That meant they had captured enemy ships for the colonial navy. The saying "Peace makes pirates" was true. When England and France ceased fighting in 1713, many privateers on both sides had turned to "going on account."

Pirates had a reputation for cruelty toward captains and crews that they captured, unless the captains surrendered immediately. By the time we decided to "go on account" the merchantmen were frightened and easy pickings. We had only to hoist our pirate flag and a merchant vessel gave up without a struggle.

We had our own code. We were very loyal to each other. The men we captured sometimes wanted to join us, and they were welcome. If a captured ship was newer or larger than the one we sailed, we'd take the better vessel and give the merchant captain one of ours in which to return home. If a captured man was married, we always set him free. But if a captive had a special skill we needed and was single, like the carpenter named Thomas Davis, we kept him, even against his wishes.

We were a brave lot. A point of honor with pirates was not to lose consciousness when an infected arm or leg had to be sawed off, or when a bad cut or wound had to be seared by a white hot axe blade!

Truth was, I didn't have much use for the rich men who both owned the boats we captured and made the laws of the colony, nor for the hen-hearted numbskulls who worked for them. It seemed to me the rich robbed the poor under the laws which they themselves had written. We pirates robbed their ships under our own laws and by our own courage. If caught, we were hanged.

In a little over a year, Williams and I captured more than fifty ships and took 28,500 pieces of eight. Then we had a chance at our biggest prize in all of the West Indies.

The *Whydah* was a huge, beautiful new ship, commissioned as a merchant slaver. It was named for the port of Ouida on the West African coast where ivory, gold and many slaves were exported. I was most thrilled when we captured her. The *Whydah* was the biggest ship any pirate had ever commanded! She was carrying thousands of gold and silver coins.

My crew was divided between the *Whydah*, commanded by me, the *Mary Ann*, commanded by Williams, and the *Anne*, commanded by a man named Noland, who had previously joined us. My *Whydah* had twenty-eight guns and a crew of over one hundred.

Now I was most eager to return to my beloved Maria. We turned sails for Cape Cod. Days later, as we neared Nauset Harbor, a huge northeaster struck. The storm became a raging gale! Our pilots tried to anchor the ship, both fore and aft. The anchors wouldn't hold. When a ship was trapped on a sandbar, I knew ships couldn't long survive the crashing waves.

What should I do?

I decided to cut the anchors' cables, but my gamble failed. Within minutes the masts were in splinters and the rigging was in shreds. Our beautiful ship's back was broken. Cows, chickens, cannons, and over one hundred and eighty bags of gold, silver and jewels were torn loose. This wildest storm pushed the ship on the shoals and ravaged her. Of the one hundred and forty-six in my crew, only two reached shore, and I was not one of them.

THE ONLY WHYDAH SURVIVORS were the carpenter, Thomas Davis, and the pilot, Indian John Julian. Davis, soaked and *freezing, with his left ankle broken, climbed a one-hundred-foot cliff and made it to a farmer's house. The Indian, John Julian, who, like Davis, had been a captive of Bellamy, washed ashore. As both were considered pirates, they were captured and imprisoned. John Julian probably died before his trial. Thomas Davis was finally acquitted.*

Barry Clifford of Orleans, a true modern adventurer, has been fascinated by the story of Sam Bellamy and the Whydah *all his life. In the 1970s and 1980s he gathered a crew and searched for the* Whydah's *remains for many months. On July 23, 1984, a telegram went out to the Underwater Archeological Resources Board, "Important: Whidah has been found."*

After locating Whydah's remains, Clifford said, "My life right now is a fantasy. What I mean is, how many people actually get to hunt for buried treasure in their lives?" And he had found it!

Clifford hopes to open a "hands on" Whydah *Museum and Research Center on MacMillan Wharf in Provincetown in the spring of 1996. He says, "People will have the chance to see these artifacts fresh from the ocean, still dripping water as we unload them." Clifford believes that his group should continue to find artifacts from the* Whydah *for at least ten years. Restoration of these artifacts will take much longer.*

Isaac Snow

MY NAME IS ISAAC SNOW. I was born in 1758 on Tonset Road in Orleans. I went to school four months each year, but my sisters couldn't go at all. Only boys were allowed in school in my day. We had two school rules: no swearing, no using snuff.

When I was seventeen, our American colonies were fighting the English because they taxed us most unfairly. I wanted to join the fighters, but my family begged me to stay home and help with our little family farm.

What should I do?

I decided to enlist with the fighters. I walked ninety-five miles to Boston to help General Washington's men. My shoes wore out, but not my feet!

Along with other soldiers, I signed up for three months. After I saw the British leave Boston Harbor, I reenlisted for six months and marched to Rhode Island, one hundred and eight miles. There I joined a colonial ship and we captured a valuable British ship sailing under a letter-of-marque. (A letter-of-marque was a government paper given to a ship that allowed her to capture merchant vessels of an enemy nation. Such ships were a kind of addition to a country's official navy.)

We managed this capture in spite of having a lot of smallpox on our ship. I also had it. Smallpox was the worst disease everywhere. Even our Cape Cod courthouses had to close for six months due to the smallpox epidemic.

Next it was my turn to be captured, by the British! I'd shipped out on another vessel, loaded with tobacco bound for Cadiz, Spain, and we were overtaken by an English frigate bound for Portugal. It was useless to resist, so we yielded ourselves as prisoners of war and were put on a prison ship.

I soon saw enough of prison life. One evening in a Portuguese harbor while the English officers were having dinner, some of us escaped in a row boat. On shore I hid in a drainpipe under the road, but was squealed on and discovered by a British officer. I offered him $1.00 to let me go free. Thankfully, this was enough and it was an offer he couldn't refuse!

I and my fellow escapees were helped by a Frenchman who was paid by the colonies to care for any American prisoners. We learned that a French fleet was forming in Brest, France to go to America and serve the colonies under the French General Lafayette. We could get home by joining that fleet and decided it was worth walking four hundred miles across Portugal and through Spain. We sailed with the 10,000 French troops and finally landed safely in Newport, Rhode Island. The French troops joined Lafayette, and I walked the hundred miles home.

Next I shipped on an American vessel with a letter-of-marque carrying freight to the West Indies, but once again a British frigate captured us and carried us to Mill Prison in England. We were condemned for "treason and piracy upon his majesty's high seas." Seven hundred men were confined with me there for twenty-two months.

We tried to escape by digging a tunnel under the prison wall and putting the sand in our mattresses and into our well. When the tunnel was complete, the fellow who had been our leader, a huge man, wished to be the first to escape. He wriggled to the end and then got himself wedged between two rocks, unable to move forward or backward. By forming a line, one man grabbed the wedged man's heels, and another the heels in back of him, and so forth down the line. Soon, we finally got him "free"—back in prison! Only two prisoners managed to escape before our tunnel was discovered. I wasn't one of them.

The one good thing about being in prison was that it gave me an education. The officers who were imprisoned taught the rest of us language, math and navigation. After almost two years, all American prisoners were exchanged for British prisoners and I returned, thankfully, to Orleans. I had been gone seven years. My mother thought I had died, and when she saw me, she fainted!

I had had my fill of sea adventures and was happy to settle down in Orleans and marry Hannah Freeman. I did a variety of things to make a living for Hannah and our nine children. I shellfished and was the fish warden. I made peat fuel from peat bogs, and also made shoes, moved houses and helped tend the

saltworks. We made salt by drying the sea water in huge flats driven by windmills and sold it far cheaper than we could using the old method: boiling sea water until it evaporated. In a year we made as much as 21,780 bushels of salt in our fifty

saltworks. I also did other jobs like mending highways, boarding the schoolmaster, and boarding the town's poor—till in 1831 Orleans built a poor house so the poor were no longer boarded around.

In 1800, along with four other men, I built a grist mill on Great Oak Road. We five shared in the work and supplies, and I was the miller for thirty-five years. We ground corn, salt, rye

and barley, all produced nearby. In 1819 the mill was sold to the Congregational minister and moved to a hill overlooking Meeting House Pond where I continued as miller.

When I was fifty-six I volunteered for guard duty at Rock Harbor. Once again we were fighting the British, in the War of

1812. Their big naval ships controlled Massachusetts Bay. The British ship *Spencer*, under Commander Richard Raggett, was the terror of the bay. Raggett demanded each town pay him $2,000 or he would destroy the town's saltworks and destroy the houses on the bay. Only Orleans and Falmouth refused to pay. Many of us depended on the saltworks for our livelihood. But we were a brave and determined lot!

A couple of British ships came into Rock Harbor and set fire to two American sloops. I had guard duty in the militia at Rock Harbor and we broke up the Brits' attempt to land there. We managed to kill a couple of Red Coats and they fired some shells into Orleans. One landed on a Rock Harbor house.

An American whale boat was in the bay, loaded with rum and captained by Matthew H. "Hoppy" Mayo. It was captured by Raggett's men. When a storm blew in, the Brits, who didn't know the bay, ordered Hoppy, who knew the bay's waters well, to pilot the *Spencer* to a safe mooring.

Hoppy gave the twenty-three Brits plenty of rum and managed to get them locked below. He then picked a lock in Captain Raggett's cabin and took his pistols. He threw the Brits' other arms overboard, ran the *Spencer* aground in Eastham, then took a small boat and headed home. The Eastham militia took the furious Brits prisoner. This capture was the best laugh of that war.

After my wife died I moved to Cobbler's Dell on Barley Neck Road to be near my son, Captain Russell Snow. I had named Russell after William Russell of Boston who was my fellow prisoner in England and who educated me there. When there was time to spare I told war stories to my twenty-nine grandchildren and twenty great-grandchildren and they loved to hear them. I died in 1856 at the age of ninety-seven. I was the last surviving Revolutionary War soldier in Barnstable County.

*I*N *1776* MORE THAN ONE-HALF *of American sailing vessels were captured by the British.*

Sixty years after the Battle of Rock Harbor Congress remembered this battle by rewarding the militiamen who fought that day, or their widows, with one hundred and sixty acres of public lands.

In 1890 Captain Joseph D. Taylor and his partner bought the East Orleans mill. He built his grand home, now the Barley Neck Inn, across the street from the mill.

Joseph's son, Mark, learned the milling trade in the same East Orleans mill. Mark then went to Boston to make his fortune and eventually, with partners, produced the famous King Arthur Flour.

In 1958 Charles Campbell bought the old mill, which was then a wreck, and painstakingly restored it. His wife Dorothy ran a small gift shop in it for a couple of years. At last, the town having refused to buy the mill, it was sold to Heritage Plantation in Sandwich. Partially dismantled, it was moved there on two flat bed trailers in 1967 and there it remains today as a choice piece of Americana.

Cobbler's Dell still remains on Barley Neck Road.

Lucia Higgins

M Y NAME IS LUCIA HIGGINS. I was born in 1774. I never knew how to read or write or cipher because girls weren't allowed in school when I was young. Our mothers taught us cooking, sewing and kitchen gardening, all we needed to know in order to get married. When I was twenty I married David Snow II.

A few years later my husband was lost in a storm at sea. He was on a schooner laden with salt fish for Santo Domingo in the West Indies. All the men went down with the ship.

I was left with three tiny children to support. The youngest was David III, only three weeks old. Usually new widows were farmed out for the price of three pounds and moved in with widowers to keep house for them. Often they ended up marrying the widowers.

What should I do?

I didn't want to earn my living that way.

I owned my house and four acres of land. I sold one acre for $25.00 and that gave me enough money to start a small store in my kitchen, which was the only heated room in my house.

My nephew had a bake shop in Boston and he brought the things I needed for my store: a barrel of crackers, a chest of tea, a barrel of molasses, a keg of rum, twists of tobacco for pipe smoking and chewing, evaporated salt, and snuff. I also carried thread, needles, pins, buttons, tapes, stationery and homespun cloth dressed at the fulling mill at High Brewster. The fulling mill thickened the cloth with moisture, then paddled and squeezed it until it was close and smooth enough for making clothing.

Perhaps you wonder how I could run a store when I couldn't cipher or read? Most of my business was done "on the cuff" or by bartering. This was how I managed my "trust" accounts. I knew the letters of the alphabet, and used a capital letter for each customer's name. On a long horizontal line I kept each account.

A long vertical line down equaled one pound.

A half vertical line down equaled six pence or one-half shilling.

A half vertical line up equaled one pence.

Here is Linnell's account for a pound of butter and a cord of oak wood. What do you figure he owed me?

Eventually I had an agent, a packet captain who shared my profits in return for bringing me items such as salt-cured fish from Boston. Although I didn't become wealthy, I was able to support my family and my children no longer went to bed crying with hunger. As my business grew, I was able to make two or four packet trips a year to Boston by myself and be my own agent.

I was also able to buy a peat swamp from the town's doctor for $50.00. Since most of Orleans wood had been cut down by the War of 1812, and coal was rarely used, selling peat increased my profits.

Although in 1800 packets could reach Boston in just a few hours, stage coaches took at least two days. I also had my goods brought by oxcart over the sand-rutted highways. Transport was expensive, but goods brought high prices: $18.00 per barrel for flour and corn was $2.50 a bushel. There was no molasses coming from the West Indies during the War of 1812, so we made a sort of molasses from cornstalk and pumpkins.

I had made a good living in my store. After my children were grown, when I was forty-two years old, I married Captain Gideon Smith Snow. As you see, I didn't have to change my last name! Captain Snow owned a saltworks at the head of Town Cove. I'm sure you can imagine that the last part of my life was easier and happier than the first.

~

*L*UCIA'S YOUNGEST SON, DAVID III, *inherited some property from his mother as well as her energy and good business sense. He eventually went to Boston and became a leading merchant in the city. He also owned a fish-packing business and became a ship owner and a banker as well. We are lucky that he didn't forget where he had come from, because he left $5,000 to start Snow Library. It was built in 1877.*

Alas, in February, 1952, the original Snow Library burned to the ground in a devastating blizzard. Sid Swan, who lived a block from the library, said his children saw a flare in the sky and called their parents upstairs to watch the burning library. They barely heard the fire alarm blowing to summon volunteers because the raging northeast wind carried the the sound of the alarm southwest toward Brewster. Only three volunteers appeared. They soon had a hose poked through the ice in Town Cove at the Yacht Club, and a relay hose at the French Cable Station. The hose pumped water and small minnows on the burning building.

Suddenly a snowplow appeared. Unable to see the hose through the storm, it ran over the hose, cutting it in two. Next morning the library was only a smoking ruin.

Joshua N. Taylor

~

MY NAME IS JOSHUA N. TAYLOR. I was born in Orleans in 1842. My family was large and poor, so when I was eight years old I signed aboard a fishing schooner as cook. We had to take our own bedding with us, and enough grub to last until our boat reached Boston. There we got all our provisions for our trip to the Grand Banks of Newfoundland.

On our fishing boat, the rust on my stove was one-half inch thick and I had to scrape it clean and grease it. Can you make fat salt pork scraps or biscuits? Those, with chocolate, were the first meal I served my crew.

We had very rough seas and I was awfully seasick for the first and last time in my seagoing days. I wanted to die. The crew made fun of me, saying, "O Cookie, take a piece of raw pork and tie it to a string, swallow it and haul it up and down; it's a sure cure."

I was *terribly* homesick. But that first trip gave me a love of salt water that stayed with me the rest of my life.

When I wasn't cooking, I was allowed to fish and was paid fifty cents a hundred for all I managed to catch. I caught twelve hundred head of fish in my first voyage.

I had a wonderful celebration on my ninth birthday—we started home! Eight days later we rowed into Town Creek. I headed home with everything I owned in a calico pillow case. I was barefoot, but I ran nearly all the two miles to my house.

In my teens I shipped with the *Red Jacket* and at twenty-two I commanded a small ship, the *Charmer*, bound for New Zealand. I made the trip in eighty-two days, which seemed unbelievably fast. One hundred and thirty-five days was considered average. My brother, Captain James P. Taylor, made the passage in his ship in one hundred and forty-five days. It is always fun to beat your brother!

We had to change the name of my ship to *Canterbury* and put her under a British flag in New Zealand. This was to escape Jeff Davis' Confederate privateers. They were really licensed pirates, and had destroyed much northern shipping during our Civil War.

Over the years I captained several ships and had many splendid voyages. On one voyage on the bark *George T. Kemp,* I became a doctor. Ships' captains had medical books in their cabins plus a few medical items such as sharp knives and needles and thread. Of course we had no medical training, still we acted as doctors when the need arose.

Captains were also expected to make a little extra money on the side in the ports where they went. For instance, while on the *George T. Kemp* in Port Elizabeth, South Africa, I bought an ostrich, a tiger, and a large vicious baboon named Jocko. Vicious, that is, toward everyone except me. I've always loved all animals and they seem to know it. We put Jocko in a big pen on deck, strengthened by iron bars on its sides. Everyone was warned to stay away from Jocko, but a big Swede named Swinson couldn't resist teasing him whenever he went by on deck. Jocko would scream, froth at the mouth and beat the bars of his cage to get at Swinson.

One noontime Swinson picked up a deck broom and started poking at Jocko, handle first. Jocko quickly hauled in the broom, but Swinson stupidly refused to let go. Suddenly there was a horrible scream from both Jocko and Swinson. Jocko had managed to fasten both of his big tusks in the sailor's throat. Jocko refused to let go in spite of my twisting his tail tightly.

What should I do?

We put an iron pin in Jocko's mouth and I cut Swinson's skin clear of the tusks. At last Jocko and Swinson were separated.

The deck was now covered with blood and Swinson was unconscious and black in the face. We carried Swinson to my cabin where we expected him to die. My mate got our book on

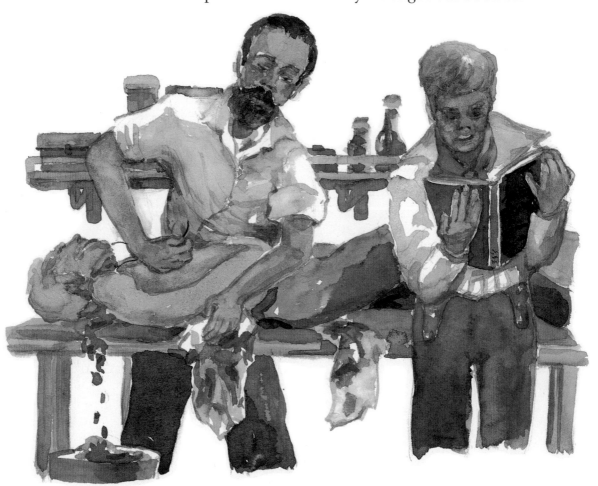

anatomy and some items from our small medical case. He read to me the neck's anatomy while I mopped the clotted blood and sewed more than thirty stitches in Swinson's neck. His wound looked very nasty.

Miracles do happen. Three weeks later Swinson was performing his usual tasks on shipboard.

When we reached Boston, a circus agent paid me $300 for Jocko—well worth all the trouble he had caused me!

One other dangerous experience with animals nearly cost all of us our lives.

Our voyage was from San Francisco to Montevideo, Uruguay. We entered the River Plate and, the wind having died, put out anchor.

As I lay taking a nap, I suddenly heard a terrible screeching and bellowing. I thought it came from the seals that covered a nearby island. I ordered the dinghy put out, and grabbed my shotgun and rifle. I thought I'd bring back seal hides to sell. We pulled toward the seals and I saw my mistake.

They were not seals, but worthless sea lions. They bellowed like lions and I fired a shot at one. Shortly, they had all entered the water and came alongside the dinghy, putting their flippers on the gunwale. I kept striking them with an iron bar and shot their leader in the face. They tried to come into the boat and I was very frightened. We kept shooting them and clubbing them and they would back off and regroup. Finally, with the sea a pool of blood, we managed to get back to our ship. I never wanted to see another sea lion as long as I lived. Perhaps I don't really love *every* animal after all!

CAPTAIN TAYLOR'S FINAL VOYAGE *was commanding the ship* Littleton *from San Francisco to Montevideo, thence to New York. Taylor said, "The old-time 'Yankee' skipper was an important factor in placing the American Flag in every known port of the world and improving the commercial superiority of its men and ships. Those times are now long past, and remain in our minds as remembrances only, of a day when American ships and American men were supreme in the maritime world."*

Taylor then retired to his home on Pond Road and grew a great variety of vegetables.

In 1995 Chauncey and Anne Williams bought Taylor's old Pond Road house. When Williams tidied up the front walkway, he lifted a stone at the end and turned it over. To his astonishment, it proved to be the headstone of Phebe Ann Taylor, Captain Taylor's sister, who died in 1851 at the age of nineteen. The poem on the headstone reads:

> *"Phebe, yet we hope to meet thee*
> *When the day of life is fled.*
> *Then in heaven with joy to greet thee*
> *Where no farewell tear is shed."*

Jack Ainsleigh

~

MY NAME IS JACK AINSLEIGH. I was born in 1909. When I was nine years old I almost died in a very exciting adventure off Nauset Beach.

My father was captain of a barge, the *Lansford*. His crew was my mother, my brother Charles, who was eleven years old, and me. My mother had been a school teacher, and she taught my brother and me while we were on the barge. We learned a

lot about ships from our father. We had a great life; lots of time to fish and swim! Whenever we were in port, mother took us to museums and historical places.

The morning of July 21, 1918 was hot and a bit misty. Our barge, with three others, was being towed by the *Perth Amboy*, a tug captained by James A. Tapley. Only one barge had a cargo, and that was granite. We were all bound for New York and were chugging along off Nauset Beach.

On that day the war the Americans had been fighting against the Germans seemed very far away.

My mother was below deck cooking ham and eggs and coffee. On the port side my brother and I were playing target practice with Charlie's new .22 Winchester rifle, his birthday present. Dad was sitting on our deck, smoking his pipe and gazing at the sandy shores of Orleans.

Suddenly German shells started whizzing by us, and before we knew it, a couple had sunk the granite-laden barge and then the one next to it! Our barge was hit and my dad was shot in both arms as he stood at the wheel.

What should I do?

Quickly, all four of us scrambled into our lifeboat. Charlie and I had grabbed his .22, plus our large American flag. Dad couldn't row with his wounded arms, so Charlie and I had to row for shore as hard as we could.

The *Perth Amboy* tug was on fire and its seventeen crewmen were also in a lifeboat. As we looked back, a shell hit our beloved barge in midships and she began to go down. My mother was crying because her home and all the things she loved were sinking to the bottom of the sea. Charlie and I were crying too, from anger, fear and sadness.

Breaking off our rowing for a minute, my brother handed me our American flag and told me to wave it as high as I could. And he located his .22 and shot toward the German sub. His shots didn't do any more harm than the bombs dropped on the sub by a couple of Naval airplanes from the Chatham Air Base. None of the bombs exploded. One pilot was so mad he grabbed a large monkey wrench from his tool kit and dropped it on the sub when the plane made its final pass over the Germans. All the other Chatham pilots were in Provincetown playing baseball.

Later I learned that the German Captain Von Oldenburg had decided to attack our barges and the *Perth Amboy* because of his own frustrated anger. His mission had been to cut the trans-Atlantic cable, which went undersea from the French Cable Station in Orleans to Brest, France. It carried important coded messages between the U.S. War Department in Washington and General Pershing's headquarters in Brest, France.

When Captain Von Oldenburg failed at cutting the cable, he was determined to find a new target. We were it as he suddenly saw the *Perth Amboy* and its four barges.

Right after our own German encounter, I learned that Dr. J. Danforth Taylor, who summered in a cottage high on Nauset Heights, was gazing at the sea through his binoculars that July morning in 1918 and thought he saw a submarine. He couldn't believe his eyes, but suddenly, sure enough, he saw it firing at the *Perth Amboy* and its four barges. He phoned *The Boston Globe* right away and gave them a blow-by-blow description of the battle, which lasted almost an hour. What a story! What a morning! From then on, no Navy airmen on Cape Cod were ever allowed to play baseball on Sunday.

The *Perth Amboy* was badly hurt by the Germans, but it didn't sink and was eventually completely repaired. Years later I was glad to learn that in our next war against the Germans, our *Perth Amboy* was one of the ships that evacuated more than 300,000 allied soldiers at Dunkirk, France, in May and June of 1940.

*T*HERE WERE MANY ACTS OF COURAGE *during the battle with the German submarine* U 156. *Captain Robert Pierce of Orleans and his crew bravely put off in a Coast Guard surf boat to rescue survivors of the burning tug. The Coast Guard's famous slogan was "You gotta go—but you don't have to come back."*

Captain Freeman of Tonset was returning from hauling lobster pots in Eastham and went into the thick of the fight to rescue survivors.

In the excitement of the battle, the dog mascot on the tug was left behind. Chatham's "Good" Walter Eldridge was bass seining nearby and rescued the dog.

Chickens were kept on board barges to ensure a supply of fresh eggs. One hen jumped onto a piece of driftwood during the Perth Amboy *battle and made it to shore. The hen was displayed in David Young's barn on Nauset Heights and one could view it for ten cents. The sign read, "See the hen the Huns didn't get." The $75.00 collected went to the Red Cross.*

Captain Von Oldenburg's submarine destroyed 34,000 gross tons of American shipping during World War I. In October, 1918, it was blown up in a minefield between Scotland and Norway.

Epilogue

ORLEANS PLANNED A GREAT DAY for its one hundredth birthday party on July 14, 1897, called its centennial. To start the day, a train was to arrive from Boston carrying Governor Wolcott, General Guild, and other state officials. The train would arrive at the Orleans station, across from Snow's Department Store.

A parade was planned from the train station to Bay View Park, home of our current windmill. Two concerts, a formal dinner catered from Boston, a regatta, a rowing race and a grand ball were to be held in the park.

Unfortunately, the weather did not cooperate! An unusual southwesterly gale with drenching downpours made the Boston train one hour late. Everyone marching from the train station was soaked to the skin.

An enormous tent had been set up in the park. Some speeches were given and one concert was held in the afternoon in spite of the rain. Then people went home to dress for dinner, the concert and the ball. The Boston caterers set up the tables and suddenly, in one huge blast of wind, the tent collapsed on top of everything! There was no dinner, no evening concert, no fancy ball.

Henry K. Cummings, a leading Orleans businessman, was born in his Grandfather Linnell's home (now the Captain Linnell Restaurant). He owned a dry goods store in town as well as half ownership in the local pants factory, which shipped ready-made pants to every state in the union. He was also an avid photographer, and many pictures of Orleans from the late 1800s and early 1900s, taken by H. K. Cummings, are now in Snow Library.

After the debacle of the Orleans Centennial Celebration, Cummings said, "The folks can have a finer celebration in 1997 at Orleans' two hundredth birthday party, our bicentennial!"

Will the weather cooperate?

Acknowledgments

~

IN HISTORICAL RESEARCH AND WRITING there are always countless people to thank, but I shall limit myself to four.

Trumbull Huntington has been the great guardian of this project. He's given steady encouragement and knowledgeable advice to all our efforts. His expertise has been invaluable.

Frances Ward Weller's charming books for young people have been a source of inspiration and she personally took time from an extremely busy schedule to read our final two versions and make most perceptive editing suggestions.

Joanne Dobson, librarian at the Orleans Elementary School, with help from her fifth graders, suggested the kinds of characters and events they found interesting. Their input started the research on its way.

Mary Sicchio, librarian in the Nickerson Room at Cape Cod Community College, is a most skilled resource person for anyone interested in Cape Cod history, as she was for me.

Finally, thanks are due to the Bicentennial Committee of Orleans for the opportunity to write this book. It has been challenging, rewarding and fun.

Sources

Bangs, Mary Rogers. *Old Cape Cod: The Land, the Men, the Sea*, Houghton Mifflin, 1920.

Barnard, Charles N. *The Winter People; A Return to Cape Cod*, Dodd Mead, 1973.

Barnard, Ruth L. *A History of Early Orleans*, Sullwold, 1975.

Barnstable County. *Three Centuries of the Cape Cod County Barnstable*, MA, 1985.

Barnstable, Town of. *The Seven Villages of Barnstable*, 1976.

Berger, Josef. *Cape Cod Pilot*, M.I.T. Press, 1969.

Blos, Joan W. *A Gathering of Days; A New England Girl's Journal 1830–32*, Charles Scribner, 1979.

Bonfanti, Leo. *Biographies and Legends of New England Indians*. Vol. 1 and 2, Pride Publications, 1968.

Boston Post, July 22, 1918. "U Boat 156."

Brigham, Albert Perry. *Cape Cod and the Old Colony*, Grosset & Dunlap, 1920.

Burroughs, Fredrika A. *Cannonballs and Cranberries*, Sullwold, 1976.

Campbell, Dorothy. *The Old East Mill, 1800–1963*, Orleans Historical Society.

Cape Codder, March 3, 1955. "One Hundredth Anniversary of Death of Isaac Snow."

Cape Cod Times Magazine, July 9, 1978. "U Boat 156."

Clifford, Barry with Turchi, Peter. *The Pirate Prince*, Simon & Schuster, 1993.

Corbett, Scott. *Cape Cod's Way, An Informal History*, Crowell, 1955.

Dalton, J. W. *The Lifesavers of Cape Cod*, Barta Press, 1902.

Dethlefsen, Edwin S. *Whidah: Cape Cod's Mystery Treasure Ship*, Marus Printing, 1984.

Deyo, Simeon L. *History of Barnstable County, Mass., 1620, 1637, 1686, 1890*, Blake, 1890.

Doane, Doris & Fish, Richard. *Exploring Old Cape Cod*, Chatham Press, 1973.

Dos Passos, Katharine & Shay, Edith. *Down Cape Cod*, McBride, 1947.

Drake, Samuel. G. *Biography and History of the Indians of North America*, Antiquarian Institute of North America, 1837.

Eastham, Town of. *Eastham's Three Centuries*, 1651–1951.

Edwards, Agnes. *Cape Cod New and Old*, Houghton Mifflin, 1918.

Freeman, Frederick. *The History of Cape Cod, Vol. I & II*, Parnassus Imprints, 1965.

Fritz, Jean. *Back to Early Cape Cod; A Story Guide for Young Readers*, Eastern Acorn Press, 1981.

Glover, Janice. *Those Billington Boys: A Pilgrim Story*, Byte Size Graphics, 1994.

Hodge, Frederick Webb. *Handbook of American Indians North of Mexico*, G.P.O., 1912.

Hopkins, Giles E. *Have You Anything to Teach Me?*, Unpublished Manuscript in Orleans Historical Society.

James, Henry J. *German Subs in Yankee Waters*, Gotham House, 1940.

King, H. Roger. *Cape Cod and Plymouth Colony in the Seventeenth Century*, University Press of America, 1994.

Kittredge, Henry C. *Cape Cod and its People and Their History*, Houghton Mifflin, 1930.

—— *Shipmasters of Cape Cod*, Archon Books, 1971.

—— *The Mooncussers of Cape Cod*, Archon Books, 1971.

Koehler, Margaret H. *Cape Cod Compass*, "The Day the Submarine Shelled Orleans," 1976.

Lincoln, Joseph et al. *About Cape Cod*, Thomas Todd Co., 1936.

Lowe, Alice A. *Nauset on Cape Cod, A History of Eastham*, Eastham Tercentenary Committee, 1951.

Morison, Samuel Eliot. *Story of the "Old Colony" of New Plymouth, 1620–1691*, Knopf, 1956.

Morse, James S. *The Story of Snow's Store in Orleans*, Shank Painter Printing Co., 1988.

Moses, George L. *Slightly Salty*, Kendall Printing, 196?.

Myrick, William P. *Mr. Isaac Snow of Orleans, A Revolutionary Soldier*, Unpublished Manuscript, Orleans Historical Society.

Napier, Rachel Baker, transcriber. *1850 Federal Census Orleans.*

Nickerson, W. Sears. *Early Encounters Native Americans and Europeans in New England.* Delores Bird Carpenter, ed., Michigan State Univ. Press, 1994.

Orleans Town Records, 1765–1840.

Orleans, Town of. *Centennial Celebration*, 1897, Orleans Historical Society.

Pratt, Enoch. *A Comprehensive History, Ecclesiastical and Civil of Eastham, Wellfleet and Orleans, County of Barnstable, Mass., 1644–1844*. W. S. Fisher & Co., 1844.

Proceedings of the U.S. Naval Institute, June 1985, Biggers, W. Watts, "The Germans are Coming."

Reynard, Elizabeth. *The Mutinous Wind*, Houghton Mifflin, 1951.

—— *The Narrow Land*, Houghton Mifflin, 1968.

Shay, Edith and Frank. *Sand in their Shoes; A Cape Cod Reader*, Houghton Mifflin, 1951.

Small, Isaac M. *Cape Cod Stories or True Stories of Cape Cod*, Reynolds Printing, 1934.

Snow, Albert E. *Readers Digest*, May 1988, "U Boat 156."

Snow, David. *From Poverty to Plenty, or The Life of David Snow*. Printed for the author by J. Bent & Co., 1875.

Snow, Edward Rowe. *Famous Lighthouses of New England*, Dodd Mead, 1955.

—— *A Pilgrim Returns to Cape Cod*, The Yankee Publishing Co., 1946.

Snow, Frederick Wheeler. *The Snow Genealogy*, unpublished, Snow Library.

Snowden, Carol. *Cape Cod Summery*, July 19, 1988.

Swift, Charles F. *Cape Cod, The Right Arm of Massachusetts*, Register Publishing Co., 1897.

Taft, Lewis A. *Profile of Old New England*, Dodd Mead, 1965.

Tarbell, Arthur Wilson. *Cape Cod Ahoy*, Little, Brown & Co., 1934.

Taylor, Capt. Joshua N. *Sea Yarns*, S.N. 1915, reprinted 1981, Orleans Historical Society.

Teller, Walter. *Cape Cod and the Offshore Islands*, Prentice Hall, 1970.

Vanderbilt, Arthur T., II. *Treasure Wreck, The Fortunes and Fate of the Pirate Ship Whydah*, Houghton Mifflin, 1986.

Vuilleumier, Marion Rawson. *The Way It Was On Olde Cape Cod*, Butterworth Co., 1980.

Wood. *Cape Cod; A Guide*. Little, Brown, 1973.

This book celebrating the Orleans Bicentennial
is made possible through the generosity of

Bank of Boston

The Hess and Helyn Kline Foundation

Thompson's Printing Company